Having received endless requests over the years to republish *One Special Summer*, and having particularly enjoyed putting together my book *Happy Times* a few years ago, I was reminded of the adventure and fun of travel and why I came to love Europe so much.

Now I live in Paris and often think what brought me to settle here. It was really because of that first trip, well recorded in this publication. Things have obviously changed a lot but the roots and rhythm are basically still the same. Therefore it seemed a very appropriate moment to go back to the beginning of my falling in love and reissue the book with a new cover and some new illustrations.

People seem to find it more and more charming. As the years pass it has become a period piece.

This was an ode to discovery, youth, and adventure by one very young.

I am deeply grateful for the joys and woes of that trip, which gave me so much insight and such pleasure in the countries I love.

— LEE RADZIWILL
2005

ONE SPECIAL SUMMER

Written and Illustrated by

Jacqueline and Lee Bouvier

RIZZOLI

ONE SPECIAL SUMMER

Written and Illustrated by

Jacqueline and Lee Bouvier

*W*e are not the Brontë sisters, but Jackie and I did occasionally put pen to paper, particularly when we gave presents to our mother—for Christmas or her birthday or an anniversary—since she far preferred something we had written or drawn to anything we might buy for her. We did this book together twenty-three years ago for her and our stepfather in appreciation for allowing us to embark on this first trip to Europe by ourselves.

I was seventeen, and my greatest dream was to go abroad as soon as I graduated from school. The main reason was that Jackie had taken her junior year from Vassar to study at the Sorbonne, and had lived with a French family in Paris. Her letters to me, of which there were many, were so full of detailed descriptions of where she had been and what she had done, other countries she had visited, how fascinated she was by the history of the places she'd seen, that I was filled with curiosity and a longing to see everything she had been writing me about.

Also, I couldn't imagine anything that could be more fun than a trip with Jackie, since we both were absolutely psychic about laughter and had the same sense of the ridiculous.

Another reason is that I believe I survived three years at Miss Porter's School only because of the inspiration of my History of Art teacher, Miss Sarah McLennan, who introduced me to and made come alive a world of such beauty that I lived for her class and was transported by the subject. At that time it was the Italian Renaissance which particularly inspired me, to such an extent that, out of the blue, at the age of fifteen I had started a correspondence with the great art historian Bernard Berenson. To my delight and amazement he replied, and ever since the first exchange of letters, one of my greatest wishes was to go to Florence to meet him.

My mother was extremely apprehensive about letting her daughters go alone on such a venture, in spite of the fact that Jackie had already lived in Paris for a year. But then Jackie had been well chaperoned and supposedly studying hard under rigid conditions. This trip would be just us and the Hillman Minx.

It took a lot of persuasion. For months in advance I talked of nothing else but the trip as my graduation present, and Jackie was dutifully convincing about how well she would look after me and how wisely she would behave. Also, she urged our mother that this would be the most exciting and impressive way for me to see Europe for the first time—under her auspices, meeting her "sensible friends," with her fluent French, etc. etc. We felt we had all arguments going for us.

So finally—at last—we were on our way!

We did this book in a state of joy and laughter, which was our mood throughout the trip. We split the fun: Jackie did the drawings, the poetry and the parts on Rome and Spain. I described most of our adventures—on the Queen Elizabeth, *in London, Paris, Venice, Rome and Florence.*

Then, happily presented to our mother with all our thanks more than two decades ago, the journal of One Special Summer *was forgotten.*

Earlier this year, in looking through an unexpected wealth of letters, diaries and old photographs for a book of reminiscences I am doing, I discovered that, since our grandfather's time, we have never thrown out as much as a postcard from a relative. My mother, after searching through her attics for material that might be useful, brought me this account of my first trip to Europe as one among several of her most precious possessions from us. We had forgotten about it. As I reread and thought about it, it seemed too much—a kind of separate entity—to include as part of my book. And so here it is, just as we did it in 1951, with not a word or a pen stroke changed.

I hope some of the fun is still there for you to enjoy!

Lee Bouvier Radziwill
New York, June 1974

A BREVIATED LIST OF VITAL DOCUMENTS

Passport
Vaccination Certificate
Traveller's Checks
Letter of Credit
Baggage Insurance
Letter to American Express, London
Letter to American Express, Paris
Letter to American Express, Madrid
Letter to American Express, Nice
Letter to American Express, Rome
Letter to American Express, Lucerne
Letter to Chase Bank, Paris
Hotel Vouchers

American Driving License
International Driving License
Receipt for Car from Jack Pry
Receipt for Car from Rootes
Customs Carnet for Car
Carte Grise for Car
International Certificate for Motor Vehicles
Car Insurance
Form for Legal Representation in case of accident
RAC Membership card
Key to RAC Roadside Boxes

AAA Membership Card
Touring Club de France Membership Card

MOTORING IN EUROPE

7 Extra Passport pictures

We stuffed these — and of course their duplicates — into our dainty purses (Now people wonder why we each have one shoulder sagging) and before we left Mummy explained their import to us and said that if we lost even ONE of them, such complete and desperate chaos would ensue that we would have to come home AT ONCE!

J, the undersigned, Secretary of State of the United States of America, hereby request all whom it may concern to permit safely and freely to pass, and in case of need to give all lawful aid and protection to

SACQUELINE LEE BOUVIER
a citizen of the United States.
The bearer is accompanied by his
Wife, XXX
Minor children XXX
XXX
XXX

Given under my hand and the seal of the Department of State at Washington MAY 27TH 19 48

Nº 218793

Passport

United States of America
Department of State

27

tion to
CAROLINE LEE BOUVIER
a citizen of the United States.
The bearer is accompanied by his
Wife, XXX
Minor Children, XXX
XXX
XXX

Given under my hand and the seal of the Department of State at Washington MARCH 21ST 19 51

United States of America
Department of State

At 9:45 pm, June 7, 1951, after pleading and pestering and praying for a year— Nº 218793 and Nº 545527 left the country.

The other "girl" sharing our cabin was 99 year old Miss Coones. She frightened me enough with her clothes on, but when she turned on the light about 4 am for the 6th consecutive time I threw back my bed curtain and was horrified to see Miss Coones' bony naked body — After that I decided I didn't WANT to know what was going on in that cabin. Telegrams arrived for us between 6 and 7 am and Miss Coones would stand by the door shouting "For Jacklyn" — "For Lee". Today we were terribly lucky and managed to get switched to a cabin by ourselves. A trip with Miss Coones would have been a fascinating experience, but a little exhausting.

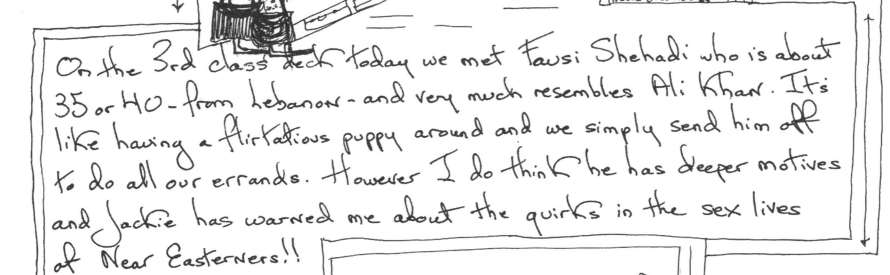

On the 3rd class deck today we met Fausi Shehadi who is about 35 or 40 — from Lebanon — and very much resembles Ali Khan. It's like having a flirtatious puppy around and we simply send him off to do all our errands. However I do think he has deeper motives and Jackie has warned me about the quirks in the sex lives of Near Easterners!!

Last night Jackie and I tried to make ourselves look respectable to sneak into 1st Class. We tore across the 3rd class deck, lept over a large fence, whizzed down 1 flight of stairs, lept over another fence — and finally we were there. I keep catching my heel in the hem of my dress which wastes alot of time. I'm sure I'll have broken every bone in my body by the time we arrive. We spend most of the time dodging officers and now have the guiltiest expressions on our faces whenever one looks at us. I have this fear that soon we'll be caught in the act — the whistles will blow — the ship will halt while we are condemned.

Cables arriving steadily every day all day long — and in turn they're going out steadily which means our money is rapidly vanishing in vast sums. It started with a cable from Mr. Bevan saying:

DINNER DANCE ARRANGED LONDON WEDNESDAY EVENING VERY MUCH LOOKING
FORWARD SEEING YOU CALL FOR DETAILS CAMBRIDGE 4410 ON ARRIVAL
                                                    BEVAN

Last night after dinner I felt I simply had to dance and informed Jackie I was about to pick someone up, when suddenly a form of humanity appeared before me known as Iganovich Illiwitz from Persia, and whisked me around the dance floor. The only thing I could see in the whole room was his nose — and then he kept trying to proudly point out his family to me. I finally realized which they were — It was the same nose on the same face of everyone of them, only it came in all sizes. Suddenly I noticed Jackie waltzing around with the purser who I had dreamt of all day. I was absolutely infuriated by this and simply repulsed everytime I had to look at Iganovich.

This afternoon a fat old woman was seasick in the same bathroom I was in, and two of her front teeth were lost in the event. She wanted me to help her find them in the last disposal, but she had apparently flushed them down the toilet with her first deposit. That really made me feel on top of the world for the rest of the day.

We were frantic — as we weren't meant to dock until 6:15pm Wednesday — but we were determined to go. We pulled all strings possible — cabled the American Express to meet us at Southampton with a car and drive us to the Hyde Park Hotel in London. The following cable then arrived from the Hyde Park:

```
           REGRET UNABLE ACCOMMODATE YOU

                                    HIGHCASTE
```

Now we were desperate. What could we tell Mr Bevan and where could we tell him we'd be. Before we had a chance to send a few more cables — one arrived from an unknown friend saying:

```
UNDERSTAND HYDE PARK HOTEL HAVE ADVISED YOU THEY HAVE NO RESERVATIONS

I AM TAKING CARE OF RESERVATIONS FOR YOU AND WILL ADVISE YOU ON

ARRIVAL WEDNESDAY REGARDS
                                    FRANCIS BRAKE
```

We had of course cabled home about every new development. Next arrived one from Uncle Hugh saying:

```
OCA 2373 · CW GXB 41 GBW / WYC 86 WASHINGTONDC
LT = JACQUELYN BOUVIER SS QUEENELIZABETH
SOUTHAMPTONENGLAND =
MRS. DUBOULAY MEETING YOU LONDON HAS ROOMS ALL
WELL AT HOME LOVE UNK +
```

Then proof from Mrs DuBoulay:

```
HAVE ACCOMMODATION MEETING BOAT TRAIN

                                    DUBOULAY
```

But we were so intrigued with our mysterious helper that we had cabled him we were placing our life in his hands — He came through gallantly with:

```
RESERVATIONS MADE AT SAVOY HOTEL STOP YOU ARE BEING MET WITH CAR

AT SOUTHAMPTON BY AMERICAN EXPRESS

                                    FRANCIS BRAKE
```

This meant we had to cable Mrs DuBoulay saying thank you very much but everything has been taken care of – to which we got a humble little reply:

SAVE FRIDAY COCKTAIL

DUBOULAY

The Telegraph boy wearily said to me today – "God – you're more trouble than anyone we've had on this ship"!!

THE

HILLMAN

MINX

WE HAD A CAR

GREAT BRITAIN WELCOMES YOU

ROOTEITAN COMPANY LTD

£500   £1500

"And what does gB mean?"

I.

We got it in London — and its weight in documents along with it

II.

At first we had a little trouble learning the gears

III.

Especially reverse

IV

But once we got on to it – it took us all over the place –

"Excuse me – Can you tell me what country this is?"

V

Until we sold it in Paris

Spanish diplomats and schoolteachers and a Yugoslavian with his 6 Mafia friends who wanted to give us the money in a shoebox, and a G.I. who we hid the dent from by parking it against a wall, came to peer and poke at it, while we stood by trying to look nonchalant. We finally sold it to Harrison Davidson Esq. who said he was a missionary but looked as if he had just escaped from Benny Goodmans String Quartet. He was going to take it to the Sahara Desert and wanted it cheap because $5. could keep an African child alive for a month and every $5. he spent on himself meant one more would starve to death. We were for slaughtering the whole tribe but his conscience would only let him starve 206 of them.

I must tell you about Chamber Music at Mrs. Johnson's. It was the most agonizing experience of my life. Mrs. J. told us Pleven and Bevan were coming and we were to arrive at 10:30. "Oh good", said Jackie, "That means the concert and a fabulous souper afterwards." All week we had been in a state about what to wear. At the last minute I asked the maid to take in my white lace dress which she did by clutching two great handfuls and sewing them up. It was so tight Jackie had to wear it. She could only get into it sideways so she looked rather strange from the front. We had no dinner and spent the evening in a frenzy of geting ready. As we clumped out the door, me in a great yellow thing of Jackies I kept tripping on, I moaned "Oh I dont even want to go." "Dont you ever want to meet fascinating people or just spend all your time with your dreary little American friends", exploded Jackie as we raced down the hall.

We stumbled up the stairs of 34 Rue de la Faisanderie after a harrowing taxi ride. Jackie had had a wad of money ready ever since Place de la Concorde. A fabulous souper my foot — They were all in the dining room still eating dinner! While 10 or 12 butlers were busily lighting chandeliers we tiptoed around the room too terrified to even smoke because we might dirty a Louis XVI ashtray.

Finally with a great roar the dining room doors burst open and they came towards us— a horde of Ambassadors, Dukes, Counts and Princes, and women with emerald necklaces clanging against their knees. They would only speak to someone if they were a notch above them so you can imagine how many spoke to us. We trotted around behind Mrs J. as she introduced us - "and here I have two Bouviers", to people who sneered at us over their shoulders. Suddenly, as I was introduced to the Indian Ambassador all wound up in turbans, I felt every article of underclothing fall to my feet. I

was panic struck and couldnt decide which was best — to walk away leaving them in the middle of the room pretending I knew nothing about them — or to gracefully stoop and pick them all up underneath my skirt. Somehow I managed not to let it be seen, and spent the rest of the evening hopping like a toad, clasping my ankles.

As we were standing behind the Indian Ambassador — I didnt dare move very far — up came my one friend, this hearty creature called Mrs MacArthur — always roaring and slapping her thigh. She slapped me and a Frenchwoman on the back and said:

"Hey, get that character, will you —" pointing to a priceless Ribera of St. Peter over the mantle, "He looks just like the Indian Ambassador they stuck me next to at dinner." I shrieked with nervous hysteria until I caught Mrs Johnson's beady eye.

The Chamber Music began. Half the room obviously knew nothing about it but would have died rather than admit it. They all put on these enraptured facial expressions — Mrs J. looked as if she was undergoing some sweet agony — forehead wrinkled slightly, nostrils dilated and a sad smile. A woman near me was beating time — rocking back and forth in her chair in such ecstasy that I was afraid she would lurch into my lap. After each squeaky little piece they all outdid themselves to think up a new adjective of praise. Jackie and I were sitting in the hall with two furious counts. I started to smoke and one of them handed me a fat gold walnut for an ashtray. It got so hot it was like clutching a live coal. Finally I could stand it no longer and gave it back to him to put on the table. You could smell burning flesh as he took it. He let out a curse "Merde" and dropped it on the floor where it rolled spilling ashes. Everyone whirled on him in horrified indignation, hissing Ssshhh — He really loved me after that.

After the music was over they passed champagne and strawberry cakes that were too big to get in your mouth in one bite and too runny to keep in your hand — and then it was time to go.

Mr Johnson collared the burned count and told him that he could have the honor of escorting the two lovely Bouvier sisters to the Hotel Continental. You've never seen such controlled rage on anyone's face. He had had his eye on this plump little blonde woman all evening. She lived right near the Johnson's and he was taking her home — Now he would have to drop her first and tear across Paris with his hated cargo. She was giving us dirty looks too and we would rather have crawled home than go with them. Having already said goodbye, we tried to sneak out quietly. At the door the butler asked us loudly if he should send for our chauffeur — We tried to flee past him to freedom and the night and a taxi-stand — but no — Thundering down the stairs after us came Mr Johnson bellowing "Where are you two going alone?" Another couple were getting into their car and he grabbed the man and told him to drop us home. We piled in in mute agony. Every 3 blocks we blurted in unison how nice it was of them to take us and we hoped it wasn't inconvenient — and they would answer through gritted teeth — "Not at all — it's right on our way." It turned out they lived in Neuilly. They dumped us and were off practically before we were out of the car.

A.s we limped into the Continental, two starved emotional dishrags — I wondered just how many more "fascinating people" Jackie had lined up for us to meet next week?

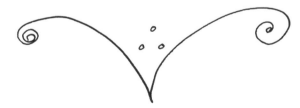

Paul de Ganay was doing his military service at Poitiers and we had promised to stop and see him on our way to Spain.

We cruised aimlessly around the town pleading out the window "S'il vous plait, ou est le 3ème Regiment 8ème Escadron des Dragons?" A truckload of cheering soldiers side-swiped us, shouting "Suivez-nous"! We were off - over rutted dirt roads, swerving as they backfired in our faces and cried "Qu'elle conduit bien, la petite!"

We drew up to a dirty yellow caserne. There was a row of soldiers on either side of the gate and someone marching down the middle. We drove gaily in and asked if anyone would possibly know where we could find L'Aspirant de Ganay. They weren't too cordial. It turned out some general was pinning on medals and we had chugged right up the middle of his guard of honor.

We fled. Someone had told us Paul's Escadron was doing Manoeuvres on a field out of town. We heard guns booming in the distance and followed our ears across uncharted regions of bumpy pasture. Through smoke and dust clouds we could distinguish foxholes. We jumped out at each one, ran belly to the ground through No Man's Land to peer in and inquire if anyone knew where we could possibly find L'Aspirant de Ganay. Leering French faces looked up at us blankly. Invitations to climb down and join them were offered freely, but no clues to Paul.

A fruitless hour landed us in a cross-fire of flame belching anti-tank guns. A clump of trees was the only haven in sight. I rolled up the windows to deflect shrapnel, crouched on the floor of the car and yelled "Come on hee - You can make it if you really try!" We careened into the clump and screeched to a stop at the feet of the 2 best looking officers this side of Paradise. They wore blue berets and had lovely gold cords twining underneath their arms. We tumbled out, patting our hair into place and inquired if anyone knew where we could possibly find L'Aspirant de Ganay. The Lieutenant smiled. I had to put on my sunglasses to intercept the ardor of his glance. He blew a whistle and 3 minutes later, trotting through the trees came the object of our search

"Paul!" we cried, and sprang for him. He recoiled and greeted us very formally. We were crushed. It would have been such fun to kiss him on both cheeks the way they do in news-reels. He stood there, a ramrod of agony and disapproval while we toed the ground nervously, wishing we had sweaters to cover up our strapless sun-dresses.

Then the Lieutenant stepped forward and saluted Paul. "Elles sont sensationelles, vos amies, de Ganay" he rolled in the tones of the Order Of The Day. "Vous êtes fiancé?" "Oui mon Lieutenant, avec les deux", Paul saluted back.

Another knee-weakening smile from the Lieutenant informed us we could take Paul away. He got in the car, we zoomed up the motor and were off into the anti-tank fire, the Marseillaise throbbing in our heads and thanking God for the North Atlantic Treaty.

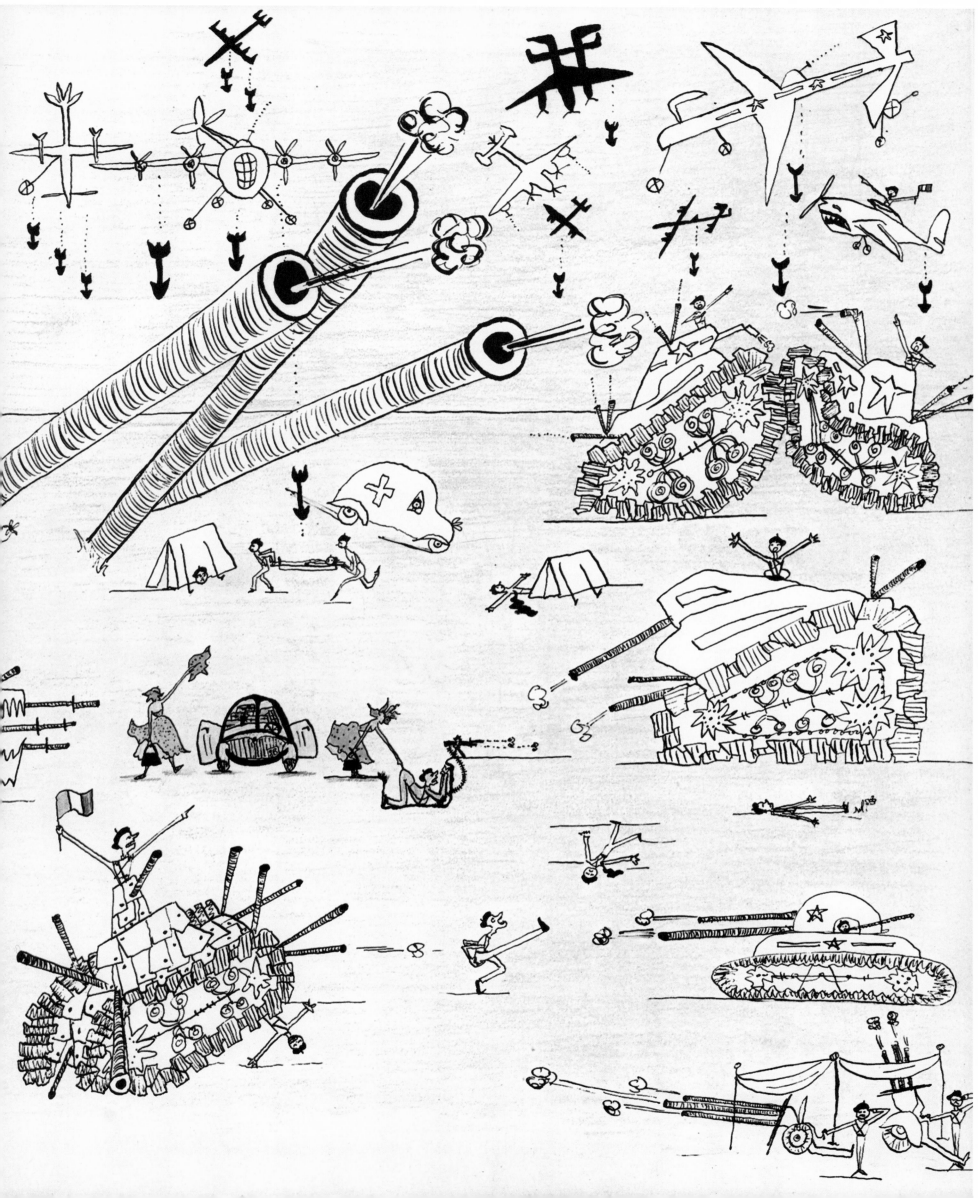

LETTERS
HOME

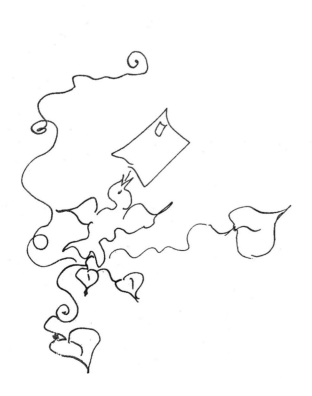

"But Inspector we really did leave our carnet in the
evening dress suitcase in Paris —
We didn't steal the car —
we promise."

Then we drove south —
stopping to see Paul at
Poitiers. We had a slight
delay at the Spanish border.
All those officials are really

so tied up with red tape —
But that gave us a
couple of days to get
to know the Basque country.

(over)

Dearest Mummy and Uncle Hugh —

If you could only know how perfect our trip is being. We cant get over it. If we haven't written you it's because every day has been so unbelievably jammed with exciting things that we just collapse into bed at night and get ready to start again in the morning. But DONT WORRY - we are not ruining our healths!

We had lunch with the Thorensens in Paris - I adore French food and we had the most heavenly things - one was soft boiled eggs in little cups — which interested me as I thought they'd serve them hard - boiled.

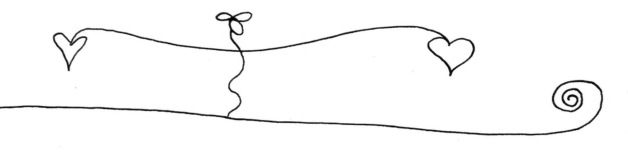

I guess you must be a little worried about us driving all over Europe by ourselves — but you really shouldn't be. We never speak to strangers ————————— and

--- everybody you've told us to look up has been so nice to us. They treat us just like their children and really seem interested in showing us their country. ⟶

And we've met some awfully nice English and Spanish boys and had such interesting talks with them. It's funny how much alike people from different countries are.

And the car is working beautifully - We only drive on good roads, in the daytime, and so far nothing has gone wrong but one flat tire on the way to Zaragossa which two awfully nice Spaniards changed for us right away!

I know you are right about us representing our country and that we must never do anything that would call attention to us and make people shocked at Americans. We DO sew on all our buttons and wear gloves and never go out in big cities except in what we would wear to church in Newport on Sundays

(over)

And we aren't just having fun – but are getting a lot out of our trip. Since we've been in Venice Jackie has really gotten terribly interested in ART. Of course we have been going to museums all along but now she seems to want to learn as much about it as she can and has found this teacher who has had a lot of experience and she takes sketching lessons from him every day.

We'll write you again soon. Give our love to Yusha and Nini and Tommy and Janet and Jamie and Soufflé – and Mummy, DON'T WORRY – We wont come home with liver trouble! We eat and drink terribly sensibly – Plenty of water and fresh vegetables.

All our love to you both

Jackie and Lee

XO

"Aw just sing her something from "Call Me Madam.""

I must tell you about my attempt to sing in Venice. Jackie was off every day scribbling with her art teacher and I suddenly felt that I must do something too. I got the most desperate urge to really learn how to sing and thought it would be such fun to run off to my little lesson every morning.

Jackie got terribly excited over the idea, saying she could come and draw pictures of me singing. The only person we could think of who would know a singing teacher was the head porter here at the Danieli — Signor Vicari. He is the most terrifying man I have ever met, with oily black hair and a wicked moustache. He treats us as if we were disobedient grandchildren and the big moment of his day is when we come creeping up to the desk to ask if there is any mail — and he can point to the empty box and look at us as if to say "Who would ever write you?" He laughed so condescendingly at my gay little idea that I decided I must convince him I had been studying for years and just needed some brushing up. I finally did impress him slightly and he warmed up and from a dirty roll of newspaper he kept hidden behind the desk, proudly brought forth a picture of his brother in law who is the greatest basso at La Scala.

He telephoned for two days and finally got us an appointment with Signora Della Rizza — Queen of all the Sopranos in Italy.

We went to her house on the Grand Canal and were ushered into this salon where we sat shaking, while the house shuddered and thundered with her singing scales in another room. On the piano was a picture of Toscanni with a long dedication to her — also one from Puccini — she was the first to sing "Madame Butterfly" — and a couple from King Umberto, and portraits on the walls of her in different costumes.

She finally came in and of course couldn't speak a word of English and hardly any French so Jackie had to interpret for us from her dirty brown Italian grammar book. She promptly asked me to sing a few arias from various operas. At that point I was so terrified I'd forgotten how to speak. My hands were icy cold with sweat and I could see Jackie in hysterics on the sofa behind her. The poor woman was so polite and finally asked me if perhaps I knew how to sing a scale. We did this one pathetic scale and my voice cracked like a sick rabbit on the last note. Jackie lolled on the sofa and kept telling me to sing something from "Call Me Madam." I knew that would really finish her off but I couldn't think of anything else except Abadaba Honeymoon. I was so frantic I decided to sing it anyway, thinking she wouldn't know what the words meant and they did sound a little bit Italian and it was so fast it might sound coloratura. I started off much too high and after three lines forgot all the words and something stuck in my throat so I ended with a screech like a cat being run over.

After that we couldn't get out of there fast enough. At the door she asked me rather worriedly just exactly what was it that I had hoped to be able to do with my voice, and I could only laugh stupidly and trip over the doorstep.

Now Signor Vicari is treating me as if I am Lily Pons' niece and everytime we pass him he asks how the lesson went. I say "Oh fine" trying to sound casual, then pretend I'm in a terrific hurry. All we hope is that we leave Venice before he communicates with the woman, or we just might be thrown out of the Danieli.

 A

Oh we're not at all what you think we are —
We've traveller's checks and a little car —
And passports we know we never must lose
We wear white gloves and we shine our shoes
But in Venice we looked for a falling star —

By a striped pole there's a gondola bobbing
Strum a guitar—add a Harlequins' sobbing
He came to our window—he threw us a rose
We slid down the vine wearing dominoes
We were Isabella and Colombine
We feasted on candy and sweet white wine,
Danced a quadrille with the Jack of Spades
Waltzed down the shadows of long arcades
I had a lover named Olio' Delmonico
And he stole a kiss by the Ca' Rezzonico
When dawn touched the top of Salute's dome
We whispered false names and we stole back home—

Oh we're not at all what we seem to be
We visit museums — each day at least three
We turn in our key at ten as I've said
But if the desk clerk thinks we go straight to bed
No one could be wronger, much wronger than he —

At Vaux-le-Vicomte Fouquet gave a ball
The lightest and brightest and biggest of all
The King was jealous — he turned quite pale
And sent poor Fouquet off to jail —
You ask who the guests of honor were?
Mais ça va sans dire — Les Bouvier Soeurs

I danced a gavotte
I ate an eclair
I looked for Lee
But she wasn't there
"Mais vous n'avez pas vu ma petite soeur?
Elle est si jeune — j'ai un peu peur —"

Yes she's taking the air
With Monsieur Molière

I did minuets
I drank champagne
Looking for Lee
Always in vain
"Mais vous n'avez pas vu ma petite soeur?
Elle est si jeune — j'ai un peu peur"

Oh she's behind the trees
With the Duc de Guise

Oh we're not at all the way we appear
We make notes of instructive things we hear
We go to church and we write our mother
We even write our sister and brother
But when night winds whisper we lend an ear.

In Florence the evenings are golden and musk
Back through the ages we tiptoed one dusk
Barefoot with our arms full of daisies and clover
We stole down Via della Vigna Nuova
We knew at the corner awaiting there'd be
Bellini for Lee and Cellini for me
On a burro we rode to the Palazzo Strozzi
Where we shortly were joined by Benozzo Gozzoli
Botticelli came in, cried "Ahi— cuesta sera
You must be the models for my Primavera."

The fresco is peeling but by peering you'll see
In the background wearing garlands coyly sit Lee and me
And if you don't believe us— why just ask B.B!

I danced a scottische
I winked at a beau
I looked for Lee
Oh where did she go

   "Mais vous n'avez pas vu ma petite sœur?
   Elle est si jeune, j'ai un peu peur."

   I've spied her running to and fro
   Blowing kisses at Watteau —

I attempted a polka
I powdered my hair
I searched for Lee
But the woods were bare —

   "Mais vous n'avez pas vu ma petite sœur?
   Elle est si jeune — j'ai un peu peur"

It's no use looking — she'll never be there
She's gone off to live on the Île de Cythère!

BERENSON

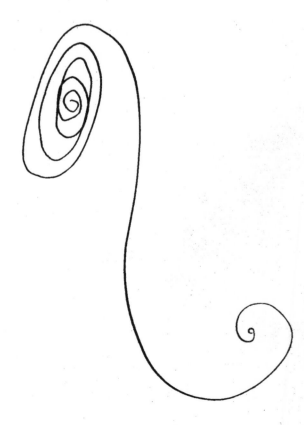

" I was born to talk and not to write, and worse still, to converse rather than to talk and then only with stimulating interlocutors. Oddly enough these are not necessarily friends. They may be total strangers or the merest acquaintances.... I delight in the glowing sympathy of the audience but I require it to participate and stimulate.... This kind of audience will not be recruited among hard-boiled, too grown up adults. We shall find it rather among individuals of whatever age or sex who remain adolescent-minded to the end."

Bernard Berenson
Sketch for a Self Portrait
April 1949

In a way it was almost upsetting talking to him. Maybe that was his intention, as he had lived every vein of life so fully and yet not thrown anything away. Every vein is still thriving and producing as that is what he is doing. He is one out of thousands and as he said, it isn't by luck or fairness but "by the indifference of God or the grace of God."

"The only way to exist happily is to love your work." He has loved and loves beautiful women and beautiful things and above all his work, which is the one thing that makes life worthwhile and complete. HE is Plato's product of "birth in beauty in order to create."

Anything you do, he could find a philosophy for. "Anything you want, you must make enemies for and suffer for," and he would so much rather make enemies than be loved by all.

We left almost feeling depressed as our visit had seemed so incomplete. We had hardly said a word and every word of his was so great and so true that if we only could have listened longer — then gone away and contemplated all of it, and choose the path from there.

He set a spark burning. It was the difference between living and existing that he had spoken of, and both of us had simply been existing in our selfish ways far too long. Maybe THAT was why it was so upsetting but more because you longed to reap out of life what he had but knew you never could.

He is such a genius, such a philosopher, such a pillar of strength and sensitivity, and such a lover of all things. He is a man whose life in beauty is unsurpassable.

A figure of slight body, white beard and brown hat was walking towards us from the woods. He made a very impressive first meeting and sat down — immediately to talk to us of love. Most of his conversation was about Life Diminishing and Life Enhancing people, the two terms he created in his last book. Don't waste your life with diminishing people who aren't stimulating — and if you find it's often you are with unstimulating people, it must be because you yourself are not stimulating.

He said, "Come back soon darlings and see me — soon." I told him he would live for years and he answered and said, no — that he didn't simply want to exist, as soon as he stopped living he wanted to die and not simply exist for years.

He said he had lived in Italy for sixty-four years and yet he didn't know her at all, as she was much too great to ever know. Once he had known Florence, every corner of her, so that parts of her were like deposited sediments inside of him, but now they had evaporated and he felt he didn't know her at all.

He is a kind of god like creature, in the way that he doesn't fit in with the hurly-burly, busy pattern of our present world. He doesn't belong — with his poetry like words and his hands like silky polished marble. He seemed the height of aestheticness without effeminacy.

Pericle Fazzini

Via Marguta

The sleepy little pink street hidden behind the taxi-tooting shopping swank of the Piazza di Spagna. We went there looking for Bill Congden and found Fazzini — and his friends who sat in the courtyard studio all day — smoking and talking while he sculpted — Romeo the poet — wild Carlo his helper — Vincent the G.I. Bill American making money as a movie extra and Teddy his wife who wanted to get back to Brooklyn. There weren't many people we knew in Rome in August and we spent most of our days with Fazzini — meeting there after our museum and shopping tours — going out to lunch en bande — an aperitif one place — melon in a garden restaurant — coffee in a bamboo-curtained cafeteria — then back to the studio — where he taught me to make ceramic jewelry in one corner and drew pictures of me in another. They were slightly more abstract than I had imagined myself — but I loved them — splotches and lines and he gave me eight. We learned his wife was dying of a bone disease and that they had a 4 year old daughter Barbara. We brought her a rocking horse and he was so touched he made us go through great piles of his drawings and choose 4 each. You couldn't stop him from giving from paying for lunches — pausing to talk to anyone who ogled in the door of his studio. He took us to a chapel he was doing in the Popes church — to a documentary of his work, and a

Jackie so plump and full of attraction
Posed for Fazzini and came out abstraction

we put his statue of a stalking cat in the courtyard and took pictures of the real cats
hissing at it... He couldn't speak English - nor we Italian but we talked together incessantly.
Such a gentle vie de Bohème — no bearded Paris cynics — When we left for Naples in our
groaning car - they all came out into the pink street and waved goodbye.

OFFiCiAL LiFE

in

SPAin

As we stood outside Mr. Griffis' office smoothing our white gloves and wondering what in heaven's name we would talk to him about, I told Lee that above all she had to remember to call him Mr. Ambassador.

We went in and he stood up at his enormous desk between Spanish and American flags and behind a picture of Truman, and said "Hiya kids, come on in!" We nearly answered "Rodger Dodger, Stan old Man."

After a very nice little talk where he asked us how were Mummy and Grampy and we asked him how were Franco and Don Juan we got up to go. He asked us if he could do anything for us, get us any cigarettes, boys to take us out or lend us any money. We said no thank you and he asked us to a cocktail party that afternoon for THE SENATORS!!................

We came in and Mrs Duke flew up to us and asked us how we liked Madrid and if she could get us any cigarettes or boys to take us out or lend us any money. We said no thank you and were introduced to Senator Wiley. He grabbed Lee's hand and kissed it loudly saying "How'm I doin' – real Spanish huh?" I was left with a Spanish newspaperman whose hair looked as if he had just finished conducting Berlioz. He told me he was working on a book about Robert E. Lee called "Mia Virginia" and had just finished a series of articles on Women in Love and if I came to his office that night he would show them to me. I turned around to grab a salted nut and heard Lee saying "But Senator Wiley I just don't see how you learn anything when you go so fast."

"Listen sweetheart", he told her, "We spend at least two days in every country we go to. We get briefings from all the ambassadors and top notch officials and then go to cocktail parties where we meet a representative cross-section of the country which enables us to size up the national situation".

"Oh" said Lee.

Another Senator whose name I can't remember except that it began with B came up and asked me if I had been to Villa Rosa, this gipsy nightclub that stays open until 7:00 in the morning – and Mrs Duke reappeared with Senator Green – 84 and doddering because he had gotten off the plane at 8:30 and gone straight to the Prado.

"Senator Green loves to go dancing, don't you Senator?" she said, squeezing his arm, "Why don't you two girls take him along with you tonight?" He looked terrified and I mumbled something about having to go now, and looked for Lee. She and Senator Wiley were still entwined on the sofa. He came with us to the door saying, "You two little ladies are Republicans, I hope I hope I hope."

"Oh yes" answered Lee, "but we thought you were a Democrat."

He laughed and said that if we ever came to Washington he would take us to lunch in the Senate cafeteria because he always liked to bring a little pleasure into peoples lives by showing them around the nation's capital.

We said goodbye to our host, the Air Attaché at the Embassy and he said it had been a pleasure for him to entertain us and if there was anything he could do to make our stay more pleasant, like cigarettes or boys to take us out or lending us...........

"Gee - Do you realize you're in Pamplona!", bellowed Ace Williams, banging the table with his fist so that the glasses jumped, and squirting a bota of red wine into his mouth and down his shirt front. I certainly did realize it. For three mornings now he had woken us up at 5:30 to run before the bulls — Lee and I staggering blindly — hoping only to be gored and put out of our misery, while he thundered along behind quoting <u>Death In the Afternoon</u>. You couldn't even blow your nose without being told how Brett had blown hers on p.64 of <u>The Sun Also Rises</u>.

Ace was travelling with three friends. One wanted to stay in Spain and write about power plants for the home town paper. Another wanted everyone to come to America. You could spot him anytime, holding a Spaniard against the wall, describing imaginary skyscrapers with one hand and saying "You've got a nice set-up here - but boy! - you should see the States. Tall buildings - Yes-sir-ree! And we don't kill animals there - don't believe in it, you know." The third was afraid of germs and women and of driving over 40 miles an hour. Once they revved the car up to 43 and he felt faint and wanted to get out. This poor creature's one dream was to see St. Peter's - but Ace had informed him they were to spend the rest of the summer on the Riviera because he had a girl there.

We ran into Ace again at Cannes and found we had been in

Perpignan at the same time. "What?"— "You didn't hear Pablo Casals?," he roared, his voice choked with pain and disbelief. "Gee, do you realize he's the greatest cello player that ever lived? Boy you should have seen that concert in the Palace of the Kings of Majorca," and he hit his thigh with his chubby fist.

Ace was without his companions that night. They all had diarrhea. He gallantly told us all the French girls he knew were busy and asked us if we wouldn't like to go to Monte Carlo. "We dress, of course" he said. "But OF COURSE!" we retorted indignantly. It took us an hour to drive there and all the way he kept exploding: "Gee- do you realize we're going to Monte-Carlo! That glittering den of iniquity! The hangout of the Gay International Set, where Empires are won and lost nightly." We got there and at the end of the ballroom were three truck drivers in shirtsleeves playing poker and sucking wet cigars. "Gee Ace, do you realize we're in Monte Carlo", we said sweetly, our voices echoing through the empty halls.

Two weeks later in Venice we came around a corner into the Piazza San Marco. There at a table with their backs to us were four figures— one bent in limp dejection over a book about power plants; another throttling a waiter and pointing to the top of the Campanile; another busily wiping the rim of a glass. The fourth had neck muscles bulging, clenched fist raised. It came down with a crash that sent a cloud of white pigeons into the air ——— " GEE— DO YOU REALIZE WE'RE IN ——— " We heard no more — only the blood pounding in our temples as we ran for the nearest dock that had boats to the mainland.

The Marques de Santo Domingo, only person allowed to walk on the town walls of Avila because he owned them, showed us his plump little Madonna which boatloads of collectors arrived daily to bid for. Lee, rheumy with cold, blew her nose all through the lecture acid at the end – hissed to me weak from exuding adjectives for both of us – "Gee – if it's worth that much money I don't see why he doesn't sell it"

Christian and Alfonso Hohenlohe took us out to El Quexigal — their house that had been a monastery in the time of Phillip II. We sat in Columbus' chair — tiptoed around tables full of crown jewels — gaped at pictures signed Love George V and just felt we should be taking notes for History of Art 105 but all they wanted to do was make Ma and Pa change the vic while we jitterbugged to "Wave the Green For Old Tulane" underneath the Flemish Primitives

THE GALLERY

DREAMS OF GLORY

Carolina, Duquesa de Bronxville

Jacqueline, Fille Naturelle de Charlemagne

SNAPSHOTS

There were pigeons to feed in St Marks Square

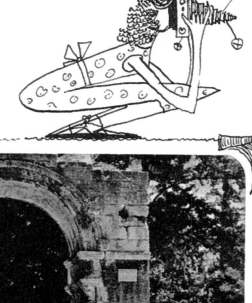

And the Alyscamps at Arles had an old old arch

Everyone else was feeding pigeons too, but it WAS scary the first time you did it —

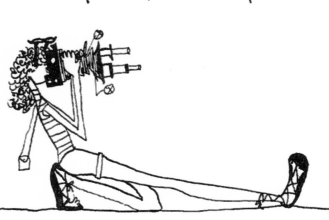

SNAPSHOTS

But then you got so that whenever you saw pigeons, you had to feed them — These are lovely white ones that lived under the geraniums at the Colombe D'Or in St Paul de Vence —

We found a mountain in the Pyrenees — where you could sit in France — and look at Spain

A latticed restaurant where you talk all afternoon

ITS ALL OVER NOW

September 15th, 1951

But it wasn't all over: it was only the beginning. We were to take other extraordinary trips together in the future. One of the most outstanding was Jackie's trip to Rome, India and Pakistan in 1961 as the wife of the President of the United States—and I went with her. Unforgettable things happened. In India we stayed with Prime Minister Nehru, possibly the most fascinating, certainly the most gentle, intriguing, sensual man I have ever met.

There were times when we were so completely exhausted by our schedule that at the end of the day, laughter overcame us as we exchanged stories of whom and what each of us had had to cope with. Then it was back to smiles and nectarine juice at the banquet table until I thought I would collapse.

But we survived, and it was great. It would have been outrageous to have missed any part of it.

In 1963, Jackie and I took another trip, this time to Morocco. We were the guests of the King, and every moment was unbelievable in every sense of the word. At one point, Jackie forced me to sing "In an Old Dutch Garden Where the Tulips Grow" to the King's harem. We were waiting for His Majesty to arrive, and were being entertained by the ladies with endless glasses of mint tea. It was one moment of Jackie's humor I didn't share when I heard her announcing that her sister had a lovely voice and would now proceed to sing.

I can only look back on those trips and think how marvelous it would have been if we had recorded them as we had this first one. Perhaps we had lost some special sense of time, in growing up.

L.B.R.

This edition first published in 2006 by
Rizzoli International Publications, Inc.
300 Park Avenue South
New York, NY 10010
www.rizzoliusa.com

Reprinted in 2006 by Rizzoli International Publications, Inc.

2007 2008 2009 2010 / 10 9 8 7 6 5 4

Printed in Mexico

ISBN 10: 0-8478-2787-9
ISBN 13: 978-0-8478-2787-9

Library of Congress Catalog Control Number: 2005939061

Designed by Marvin Israel and Betti Paul
Cover design by Headcase Design • www.headcasedesign.com